The Dark Side of Amazon FBA:
The little Tips and Hacks you need to know to have a profitable Business

By Malik Johnson
©Copyright 2017 WE CANT BE BEAT LLC

Copyright 2015 by Malik Johnson.

Published by WE CANT BE BEAT LLC

Krob817@yahoo.com

Table of Contents

Preface 4

Introduction 6

Chapter 1 Understanding Amazon 10

    The Amazon Customer 12

    The Ideal Product 15

Chapter 2 Sourcing 20

    Price Control 20

    Suppliers (Beyond the ones you can think of) 23

    FBA vs MF 26

    Outsourcing Virtual Assistants 27

    Saved the Best for Last 31

    Final Thought on Sourcing 35

Chapter 3 Strategies for Expanding Your Customer Base 37

    SEO Strategies 39

        Google SEO 41

        Amazon SEO 43

Chapter 4 Hacks to Rank Better 50

    Fine Tuning Titles 53

    Focus 54

Chapter 5 Feedback and Ratings 55

Chapter 6 Customer Loyalty Secrets 58

Conclusion 61

Preface

Amazon does for you what no other distribution channel can – no, it doesn't just put your product in front of millions of customers. What Amazon really does is give you the opportunity to relieve the customer's concerns about fulfillment – that's a huge hurdle. I mean, think about it, would you fork over a hundred bucks or more to some no-name business? If you are selling items that are five or ten bucks, then maybe that's not a big deal, but if you want to hit up the items that will make a difference to the bottom line, you have to go after customers who are going to make that happen.

When you use FBA, you are leveraging Amazon to your benefit. It's a symbiotic relationship that leaves you on the better end of the deal. Trust me. There is no comparison when it comes to pushing products through Amazon's platform.

Getting products on that platform is one thing, but actually being successful and making money – lot's of money, sounds too good to be true, but it is a reality. But still, it's not a sure thing – because there is one make-or-break-variable in all this - You! You determine what you do with all that retail fire power. You determine what to sell, how to price it and when to add more.

You are going to do a number of things better than the hundreds or thousands of people who are using FBA and make sure you get your product in front of your customers on a number of marketing channels including Amazon's own search engine as well as through other ancillary online sites that you can channel your customers to.

This book is designed for the novice who understand the FBA world enough to know what it can do for him/her, but not enough to know what needs to be done that can leave the competition in the dust. That's what we are going to do here. This book is about taking a new look at how you can turn conventional wisdom and turn it on its head with proven ideas and strategies to make it big on Amazon.

Introduction

To get you started the book is going to take you on a journey to understand the real elements behind the FBA model. If you are still not sure what FBA is, it just means Fulfilled by Amazon. To the novice, it just means that Amazon warehouses your stuff, and sends it to the customer that bought your product. In actual fact what it really is that you have placed your product in Amazon's inventory management system across their warehouse assets.

It's a great tool for management if you ask me. They hold the cost on the warehouse development and maintenance, and you take care of the inventory. It is a revolutionary idea and at the base of it, it just means that they are a warehousing and shipping company rather than a seller of anything. But look how cleverly that is not what the brand is known for. Overall, Amazon has had a brilliant strategy from inception to their place in the ecosystem of global retail.

Amazon has three things going for them. The first, of course, is their brand equity. Who do you know is going to look at a product coming from Amazon and say that there is a risk of burning the money they paid for it? I'd safely say that number is zero. Amazon's brand equity is soaring and it does not look to take a dip anytime soon.

Second, Amazon has a large and loyal customer base that keep going back to buy things. There is a loyal customer base and there's a growing list of customs (who eventually turn loyal). They trust Amazon (and that relates to Amazon's brand equity). Not only is Amazon's customer base global in scope, they have reached a state of critical mass in terms of loyal customers and products offered, and that has made all the difference. Why would you want to reinvent the wheel by just selling to a small neighborhood and trying to build your own website to sell to the world? The site is already there, the customers already know the URL, the patterns of buyers are well known, you just have to get on board. There is nothing to reinvent here.

Finally, Amazon has a brilliant infrastructure supporting the business. They have state of the art inventory management systems, delivery management systems and they have tracking management that is second to none.

They spend more than $1.5 billion annually on shipping costs alone. They have more than 15,0000 robots in their warehouses. They employ more than 340,000 staff globally.

When you put this all together, you have to start to wonder what it would take you to be able to do all that if you wanted to go it alone. It would be ridiculous to even try. There is no need to reinvent the wheel and instead, you could spend the energy on getting your product – whatever you design and build, or you get from a white label supplier.

Amazon even gives you the choice to have multi channel sales. That means you can even sell through other channels like eBay or Newegg or your own web store. But in those cases, you would have to provide customer service yourself and the pricing is a little different.

If you are getting goods from a supplier, or you intend to, there are a couple of ways you can get on top of things to increase your margins. We have an entire chapter on that.

There are also some things you have to watch out for. There are pitfalls that will swallow you whole if you are not aware of them. So make sure you pay attention to those later in the book.

So if you're ready, here we go.

Chapter 1 Understanding Amazon

Before you find any the right balance of motivation and awe to push you forward in moving forward with FBA you need to keep in the back of your head that Amazon has over 300 million users. To put that in perspective, that is almost every man, woman, and child in America. They have more than 30 million people who use their mobile app. So that is on the buy side and you are probably a buyer on Amazon as well.

If you are planning to sell using Amazon then maybe what you should consider is that more than 100,000 sellers made $100,000 in 2016. That could be you if you play your cards right. All those visitors and users spent 136 billion Dollars on Amazon in 2016.

Whichever way you slice this, you should want to get in on that action if you are thinking about selling your product. What you must understand about Amazon and the size of the market and following is not limited to just awe the numbers invoke. What those numbers should tell you is that there is critical mass in these numbers and that means that there is a huge variety within the tastes of the varied clientele.

That also means that you could just sell about anything to anyone. That's what most people don't get. The see Amazon everywhere and they seem them as just another brand. If you want to become as successful as the million-dollar earners on Amazon, that's the first mistake you have to overcome. Amazon is not just another brand. Amazon is the bridge to 300 million users worldwide (and growing) who, together, present a wide variety of tastes that you can fulfill. For a retailer that is a dream come true.

If you think that using FBA is an expensive endeavor, then you need to examine your motives. If you are a niche that uses white-label products and drop shipping supplies, then FBA is not the correct avenue for you. But on the other hand, if you own your inventory, either by virtue of manufacturing it or by purchasing it and taking ownership, then the option to get your items Fulfilled By Amazon starts to make a whole lot of sense.

Let's be clear about what FBA is before you can use all the pointers, secrets and hacks that we present in this book.

FBA – or, Fulfilled By Amazon just means that you own the product – almost any product, but you send it to Amazon's warehouse for storage (and they have a few located around the country, and around the world, for convenient shipping). When someone orders that product on Amazon's site, Amazon ships it out to them directly.

You come out ahead from this formula because it saves you the hassle of shipping to the end customer, it saves you the hassle of organizing and up keeping storage and it saves you the hassle of dealing with returns and restocking. There are more benefits than just these and we will cover those shortly. But for now, some explanation and elaboration on the first three will serve you a great deal.

You will see in the following chapters how to analyze your own situation and determine if FBA is optimal for you and if so what would the best strategy to take be.

The Amazon Customer

Before you can make a decision to sell on Amazon, you would have to understand who you are selling to. The typical Amazon customer can be divided into two groups. The first group is the one that comes under the Amazon

Prime label. These are the customers who have paid an annual fee and in return, they get 2-day priority shipping of any all their orders for free. The second group of customers is the one that falls outside this umbrella.

As of the end of 2016, there were more than 30 million Prime customers, approximately one for every ten US citizens. This is something that you need to take a long and hard look at. Amazon Prime is an annual membership program costing $99 (you can also get it for $10.99 on a monthly basis). In addition to the free 2-day shipping, they also get free e-book downloads, free video streaming, and music downloads. They also get occasional upgrades to one-day shipping and extra offers during the holidays.

While Prime members only represent 10% of the total Amazon customer base, they spend an average of $1600 annually versus the other 90% who average about $600 annually. What this tells you is that you have an inherent insight into the spending patterns of your customer population. Those who are also in the Prime membership tend to spend higher per unit than those not in Prime.

This gives you valuable intelligence as to who and how to target your products.

When you take a look at any page on Amazon, you will also notice that there is no way for potential customers to contact you - the seller, to ask questions. There are two competing opinions on this. The first is that it makes life easier for you since people already know what they want and they are not going to come asking silly questions. (You will tend to get a lot of that at sites like eBay where the average sale price is much lower.) The second is that because people don't have a forum to ask the seller questions, you are going to have to put a complete description on your page or you are going to have to have your own site that explains everything fully and then send the buyer to the Amazon page. There are different ways you can work this out. But the point here is that the customer you are targeting to is higher up on the sophistication scale.

Different products attract either groups differently but you are not forced to decide which product you want to target to who - all of them are available to any customer. The reasons you want to know the preference of your potential customer is to know that the Amazon marketplace is not price-sensitive, this is especially true for Prime customers. Since they are already in the frame of mind that they do not need to pay for shipping and their typical psychology is not one that is price sensitive. Research has also shown that they do not mind paying a little more for the products they purchase

The key that you have to understand when it comes to FBA is that you can charge slightly higher, for a given product and not have to worry that the customer will move on to the next seller.

The Ideal Product

The ideal product is one where there is strong demand and large margins on the product and that strong demand translate to price stability and faster inventory turnover. This is the product that you want to identify and be a part of but it is not always going to be the case. I mention this here so that you can understand the profile of the ideal product. From here on you can adjust to market forces. The worse kind of product there is - and you don't want this, is the kinds of product that has low margins and slow turnover. This kind of product opens you up to other types of risks and ties your cash up and costs you potential profits (opportunity costs) because you could have chosen products that have a higher demand and move faster.

When you think of FBA, you want to be able to sell items that benefit you. Weight the products that sell well and find a way to get them at the lowest cost so that you have higher margins. When you deal with FBA, it is a time-tested strategy that you keep your acquisition cost low. One good way of doing that is to buy in bulk and make sure that you receive deep discounts. Always pay in cash so that you can get the best discount.

One strategy that comes to mind for this is to scout around Amazon itself and look for a product that has the greatest disparity between the most expensive and the most inexpensive. Look for the seller that is taking the low-cost strategy but does not have a large inventory. Purchase this product and reprice it to a higher level. The reason you can do that is that you can leverage your marketing strength and extract better returns. The person selling at the lower price is most likely hoping that the lower price will attract customers – no it won't. That is an eBay strategy. At Amazon, that strategy has no way of working because Amazon does not list search results as a function of price. However, they do offer the user an option to choose who the results are displayed. One of the choices is to list them based on prices going from low to high. But that doesn't work the way we functionally hope for either because when you chose this option, and this happens everywhere, is that it lists most of the products that do not have any relevance to what we are searching for.

This strategy works because you get to purchase the lowest priced items and then put it in your store for the highest price. Do you know why that works? It works because Amazon is not about selling at the lowest price, it's about selling to the widest audience. It's a numbers game. The wider the swath of people you can reach the better your performance is going to be, it doesn't matter what price you sell it for – within reason.

This is where it becomes profitable to target prime customers because right from the start, you are able to charge higher and that increases your margins. But the one thing that is a rule in retail is that you have to pay attention to him much you paying for the product and not so much how much you are selling it for. What you sell the product for would be a function of market prices and demand, as well as the target demography you sell to. But what you buy the product for would also be a function of your negotiation. The more you can negotiate the price, the better profits you can hope to make. The old adage among Amazon sellers is that the profit is locked in at the point you purchase the inventory.

The reality of pricing products with high margins, targeted at higher paying customers, and getting them at low prices, automatically outlines the profile of the product for you. You can't choose a product that is easily available because that means that the price is not going to be too high and that consequently means that the margin will not be too high either. There is a balance that you have to find. This balance between volume and margin is constantly shifting and you have to find that all the time. Therein lies another lesson about Amazon – you have to be nimble on your feet and you have to be able to source for good that can take advantage of price fluctuations.

One secret to making money on Amazon, even for those on the smaller scale of things, is to be able to find products that you have in your vicinity that is below the national average in price. Depending on where you are, that could just be about anything. So, what you have to do is keep track of the prices that are out there. The other option you have is to sell things that you make yourself. So for instance, if you are making jars of jams or you make some kind of toy, or you have pillows. You could then control the pricing with more flexibility.

These are all just example to show you how the Amazon system works and the kind of mindset that you need to have to be able to make money on Amazon.

As a recap - you want to be able to get a product that is lower in cost, but you will be able to sell it at higher level and not seem over the top to your customers. However, remember that pricing is not your main driver – cost is. The lower your cost, the higher your returns. The lower the cost, the wider the market you can target. The lower the cost, the more options you have in case of price and market fluctuations. It's always about the cost, never about the price.

Chapter 2 Sourcing

We touched a little in the previous chapter about the process of sourcing for products to sell on Amazon, especially under the FBA program. If you look at it, you will realize that this is sort of a retail arbitrage. What you are doing is scouring the neighborhood, or anywhere for that matter, to find products that are cheaper than what is available out there and making the difference between the price you buy it for and the price that it is selling for on Amazon. Yeah, there are apps for that too, and I will tell you about that just a little further down.

Price Control

Continuing from the last chapter about prices and cost: The thing that you have to be sure of is that you can find cheaper products to sell. Cost is your determining factor in whether this endeavor of yours on Amazon is going to be profitable. You need to find the product that gives you the most arbitrage opportunity and have that fulfilled by Amazon for greater impact, especially if you are new to the game. Here are the three things you need to look for when you are trying to source for products to sell that have the best arbitrage opportunity.

1. Bargain items from closeouts, overruns, discounts, rejects and discontinued lines.
2. Purchase from lower cost countries where prices are lower
3. Purchase directly from manufacturers at wholesale prices

This is where the hard work comes in but it will all be worth it. For the first method listed above, all you have to do is compare the bargain item that you find from all the garage sales and bargain shopping that is out there and compare them to the prices of what is selling on Amazon. To help you do that, and to choose the product, what you can do is get an app (there are a few in fact ranging from free to about fifty bucks) but once you get the hang of it, the fifty bucks is a bargain when you realize the value of making correct decisions. The idea is to be able to shop directly for stuff that is conclusively cheaper than what is in the market at the moment.

It is fairly simple to just load the app on your iOS or Android device and when you are at the store just scan the barcode label. It will instantly show you what is comparable on Amazon. From there you can see what price differences there are, if any, and go ahead and make a decision to purchase the item. You will also be able to see what the other competitors are selling that item for. Now you can do this to just about anything out there. You can even travel to a town that has cheaper stuff and makes the purchase. You can also go to countries where the exchange rate is more favorable and the items are at a lower cost and an advantageous exchange rate. Then ship it back to Amazon's fulfillment center.

One of the things that I do when I source for my products is that I (well, I have Virtual Assistants to do that) scour local online retailers in numerous countries to see what they sell and how much they sell it for. When I have a good idea of the costs involved, I make the decision to purchase it and have it shipped to me where I repackage it and send it to Amazon.

There is nothing wrong with doing this. In fact, when Amazon first started off, that's exactly what they did as well. When someone ordered a book from them, they would order it from a retailer, have it shipped to their office and then repackage it and ship it to the customer. You are not doing anything different.

But remember the point is that you do all this so that you can keep your costs low and your margins higher. Take it for someone that has been in the retail business for some time: All this extra effort to find and purchase things that cost less is what is going to make all the difference in your bottom line. Even if you buy a bad product, if you buy it at a cheap enough price you will still walk away with some profit, or at least with limited loss.

Suppliers (Beyond the ones you can think of)

There are at least three places you can source for full-time suppliers that will set you up to sell on Amazon.

1. Online Liquidations Centers
2. Physical Liquidation Stores
3. Factory Over runs

Online Liquidation centers are all over the country and the convenience is that you can get them even when you are just sitting at home. Just do a search on your favorite search engine. Most of them will ship pallets or containers of the things you purchase to wherever you ask them to – including Amazon's warehouse. If you take a mixed lot, then you will have to sort it yourself and for that, you will need them to send it to you directly. If on the other hand, you purchase containers (40 ft shipping containers) worth of stuff and they are all packed nicely and sorted, then you can opt to have them sent directly to Amazon.

On the other hand, if you go to physical liquidation centers then this can get a little more interesting. There are a number of these shops around any given city. They get their inventory from larger stores that have discontinued an item or have moved on to something newer. This happens more than you imagine. Have you ever been to the store to get your favorite mouthwash and suddenly they do not carry it anymore? We've all had that, if it's not mouth wash its toothpaste, if it's not that, it's something else. The thing is that all those things that have been discontinued probably have a following out there and those guys typically go and check if Amazon carries them. You have an instant winner in those cases. You can use the same app to check if there is something similar or identical in the store and what pricing you can get out of it.

Once you have found competing products you can also see how they are ranked. Just because someone is selling them doesn't mean that the product is moving. No point if you buying something and stock it up but they are not selling as fast as you need them to. Be prepared to spend between $3,000 to $5,000 at the liquidation store. Anything more than this and you will be tying up your resources (cash) and anything less and you will probably not have the critical mass to be able to make a profit that means much.

When you chose these products, make sure that you get a wide variety of products unless you are certain that all $5,000 worth of widgets are going to sell in a reasonably quick fashion.

The reason you want to be able to diversify your product purchase is so that you get a better risk mitigation strategy. If you do well on half the stuff you buy and the other half is slow to move, at least you do not tie up your entire budget. So remember these three rules when it comes to suppliers:

1. Buy in bulk so that you can drop the price even further from the already discounted prices. This

gives you better margin and better recovery of capital.
2. Diversify your suppliers so that you can find a wider variety of items and sell them to a wider variety of customers.
3. Build a relationship with suppliers and have them send the stuff to Amazon directly so that you can keep your costs low. If they send it directly then you will be able to only incur a one-time shipping cost. If they ship it to you and then you have to ship it to Amazon, then you will have to incur the cost twice. So be smart, send it directly whenever possible.

FBA vs MF

This book is about FBA, but I want to make sure you know that there is not just one avenue for you to be able to maximize your reach and profits. There are some products that do really well when it comes to selling them and having Amazon fulfill the orders. When you are new that is a great way to do it because the buying public trusts Amazon. Amazon has powerful brand equity that you cannot compete with and since you can't beat them, you might as well join them and make it work. When you do it with FBA, there are certain stocking and shipping costs involved but the headaches are significantly less. Some products just do not lend themselves to FBA, and so for this, do not leave out the possibility that you can still sell items that are merchandiser fulfilled. It would be ideal if you did this after gaining some record of accomplishment with your products and service.

In the final analysis, it should not be that you have to choose one or the other, you should have both at your disposal and use them when appropriate.

Outsourcing Virtual Assistants

This is a secret that you will not find in many places. There are a number of successful sellers who use this but they don't really talk about it. If there is nothing else in this book that you learn. Make sure this is the one that you do follow.

One of the best ways to make money on Amazon is to be sure that you find the products that are cheaper than what others are getting – we have covered that conceptually. In practical terms, here is how you should do it.

When you keep your overall costs low and you keep your prices at the same level or higher (slightly) than what your competitors are selling, you start to see that it makes strategic sense in addition to financial sense. Look at it this way: For every dollar they make, you will make more. In the short run that does not seem like much, but that advantage compounds in each cycle as you advance. That gives you resources to increase your inventory and increase the size of your operations.

Here is how that works if you invest in an inventory that is selling for $10. Your competitor is buying it for $5 that means that he is making a gross profit of $5. Let's leave out shipping and forwarding and all that stuff because that is constant.

If you, on the other hand, manage to find the same identical product for $3, then you have a gross margin of $7. For every $5 he makes you make $7. So for one batch of 100 units, he makes $500, you make $700. If you both roll those profits back into product then he will have $500 to spend on new inventory and you will have $700. If he is getting at $5 that means he buys 100 units. If you are buying at $3 then you get to buy 233 units. The second round of sales at the same prices yields another $500 in profit for him, but $1631 for you. That's more than triple what the other guy is making. The competitive advantage of cost control is significant so make sure you adhere to the adage that profits are made when buying, not selling.

So let's get back to outsourcing. When you outsource some of the work, what you are doing is attempting to take advantage of foreign pricing discrepancies. The same product will never sell for the same price in different countries. And since, by definition, the entire exercise of selling on Amazon is indeed retail arbitrage, you will be doing the same thing here except across borders. Granted, you shouldn't do this with some products especially ones that involve technical assistance and after sales service. But for one-off sales where any deficiency in the product can be easily remedied by a refund or a replacement, you can sell very easily.

What you need to do is hire Virtual Assistants. You then need to equip them with the app that compares prices and have them scout for products in third world countries. Let these virtual assistants who work for $2 an hour go out and source for your products at third world pricing. As an example, my VA in Thailand found me a container load of 300-count white fitted sheet sets. There were selling for BHT30 per set and there were 600 sets in the container. BHT is the Thai currency and that works out to be just under US$1. The entire container cost me $540, plus shipping back to the States was a little more than that. In the end the cost I incurred, including my flight down to Bangkok and my time there was less than $1800. That averaged out to $3 per set, which I sold for $16.99. My inventory cleared in less than three weeks. My gross profit for that exercise was over $8,000. While I was in Bangkok I did a little more shopping and put that up on Amazon as well. My VA received a $300 bonus. The only reason I went down to Thailand for this transaction was that this VA was new and I had never worked with him before. Since that time, whatever he finds for me, I just wire the money to him and he does the transaction there.

This is why outsourcing is important. Not all of them will find good deals all the time. Nevertheless, you will find good deals over time and as time goes, you just equip them with the app to compare pricing and you pay them based on profit and a daily wage that works out to be a few bucks a day because of the exchange rate. You still come out way ahead. This is one way to employ Virtual Assistants, but there are other functions that you can engage them for including content creation for blogs, blog design, website authoring and much more.

Saved the Best for Last

Once you get your hands around simple outsourcing like we have above, now it's time to get into the big boys game; and here it is. The one thing that you will have to do to be able to make significant leaps in your ability to advance your FBA business is to be able to outsource your production and manufacturing of goods from China.

If you don't know how this works then you need to pay attention here. Politics aside, China makes just about everything under the sun, and they will make anything for you as long as you pay them to – and you won't have to pay too much. All you have to do is ask. To be able to outsource from China there are a number of ways that you could do it and I will get to that in this section. But first, let me paint you the picture that you need to see.

China is the current world's manufacturing powerhouse. However, there is one major oversight that most people have when it comes to China. What they do not realize is that after years of growth, China started to slow down in 2016. The major issue that this caused was that there was a significant overcapacity by the sudden slowdown in activity. From 1990 to 2016, China had continuously invested in factories that made almost everything you could think off. From cars to computers, from pots to oil rigs. With the sudden tapering of demand, all that excess capacity has started to cause falling numbers in the production and manufacturing sector. This is good news for whoever wants to manufacture their own goods. Whether you want to make rubber hoses or camera cases, China is your best bet, especially now while there is idle capacity in many of China's manufacturing centers.

If you want to seriously take the FBA game by storm, then you need to be able to source for existing goods efficiently and whenever possible you need to be able to go out and manufacture your own. If you can do that then the goods are shipped directly to fulfillment centers that Amazon owns across America and in Asia, Europe, and the Middle East. If you can do this, you will be able to keep your overheads low, without ever needing to spend a cent on manufacturing infrastructure and you wouldn't have to hire even a single person to take care of your shipping, inventory warehousing and restocking efforts.

There are sufficient resources for you to hack the entire system and be able to manufacture what you want for pennies on the Dollar for most goods. You can sell anything from watches to handbags if you are willing to go the distance.

If you are hesitant because you don't know how to get started, guess what? You already have. The fact that you are here and you are getting the information puts you on your way. Your next step is to get on line and find when the next manufacturing trade show is going to be and where it's going to be held. It will most likely be in Singapore, Hong Kong, Shanghai or Beijing. Even though the show may be in Singapore, it will be filled with representatives from China trying to give you the best deal they can. Their fierce competition will work in your favor. The best of all the shows to go o is the Global Sources in Hong Kong that is held typically in the fall.

Another good way to find suppliers and manufacturers is to search on Alibaba.com. This is one of Asia's top online B2B marketplaces and you will be able to find almost anything you need. One of the biggest secrets that is hiding in plain sight is that more than half, and almost three quarters according to some estimates, of the goods that are sold in FBA, are manufactured in China and have been sourced through either Ali Baba or one of the other B2B portals.

If you have smaller products in mind, you may not even need to head out to Hong Kong, you may well be able to get them to send you samples that you can pay for. If the samples meet your needs then you should proceed with caution and make a small order for the first round. When you do make the order, do not pay for shipment up front. You should always use a bank and pay for the order using an escrow or using a Letter of Credit that is drawn on an international bank. That way, if the seller does not comply with the specification set out in the purchase order, the payment will not be credited to this account.

You must take these precautions, not because they are out to cheat you or get to you, but because there is a lot of misunderstanding that can happen between what you intend and what they comprehend.

There are a number of trade banks that you can use to be able to pay a Chinese supplier. If you are not sure, check with your personal banker. Alternatively, there are a number of international banks located in major cities across the US, From New York to Chicago, to Los Angeles. You should not have trouble finding a bank especially if you are willing to pay for the instrument in cash and you are not taking out a loan or facility to complete the transaction.

Typically, your first transaction with manufacturing your own product should be in the region of about $10,000. If you take your FBA business up step by step, then you

Final Thought on Sourcing

Sourcing is an important part of your success story when it comes to doing well in retail arbitrage and selling on Amazon. Remember the biggest advantage you have is the ability to connect with people who are willing to spend $1600 per year and who are sophisticated shoppers. You just need to focus on what they are looking for and what they need and you will be well rewarded.

The one point that I must caution you about is to not jump from zero to manufacturing in one leap. You need to take your time, whatever that may be. For some people that is 6 months, for some people that's 4 years. You need to work out the period for yourself because you need to learn and get a feel for the market yourself. Amazon is just your conduit – you need to learn about the people making the purchase.

You should also know that language could be a problem when it comes to negotiating simple contracts. This is also why you need to outsource the hiring of a competent VA who can speak the language. It does not need to be a lawyer – just someone who can translate things for you when they are speaking amongst themselves and who can translate written documents for your understanding.

Chapter 3 Strategies for Expanding Your Customer Base

This chapter is based on common sense acts that you should do as a matter of course. Nevertheless, in the pursuit of being thorough, let me lay out the strategies you need to keeping your customers and advancing your customer count by aggressively and continuously promoting your sales beyond just the Amazon product listing.

Many people, especially the ones who fail at trying to make FBA work are guilty of the following three sins:

1. Not going after new customers
2. Not actively trying to keep the old customers
3. Not expanding their product offering.

If you just want to sell to the customers that randomly pop by your page, then you are going to be sorely disappointed with this endeavor. It is true that there are 300 million users on the Amazon website. It is also true that the 30 million Prime customers are constant buyers. But that is not enough to guarantee that you are going to make top sales the first month you open your virtual shop.

You need to actively get customers to come over and visit your page and you must not rely on Amazon to do that for you. Amazon uses its own proprietary search engine and it is based on a number of factors and it is highly unlikely that the newcomer on the block is going to get any favorable treatment for any length of time when the first get started.

So what you have to do is split things up for a start. You first need to actively go after customers. The second you must make sure that customers come back to you when they are looking to refill or looking to buy a similar product that you offer. The first one is a little easier to do while the second one can be a little harder.

As such, the question now becomes - How do I target new customers?

I have looked around for books and blogs, advice and chatter, for anything that can teach the novice how to actively target and sell to customers on Amazon. What I found for all my trouble is that every single one of those sites I read focused entirely on how to get supplies and how to get into Amazon. Not many, in fact, not even a few could come up with a credible plan to target and pursue customers actively.

And here is the reason why. Because you don't need to. When you have a market that is 300 million strong, and when that market spend $600 per year per person across 90% of them, and when the remaining 10% spends $1600 per year, what you realize is that if you are on Amazon, someone's going to show up to buy your product.

What you have to do is keep it together. And find the product that everyone is looking for and the product that you are certain that customers will buy. You can back-up your Amazon efforts by supplementing SEO strategies and create sniper pages when you get people to come to a landing page and then take them to your Amazon listing. How to do that is next.

SEO Strategies

There are three ways that you keep revenues increasing one quarter to the next.

1. The first is that you keep the old customers by keeping their contact
2. The second is that you cross sell them from one to the next
3. You gain new customers who are looking for the product.

It has been proven time and again that 60% of online buyers first go to Amazon to search for what they are looking for. So the strategy should be to concentrate your efforts on Amazon, right? Wrong. The strategy is not to just stick to Amazon, it is to diversify your efforts. You shouldn't just place all your eggs in the Amazon basket when it comes to pushing yourself forward.

There are two fronts that you have to pursue. One is the existing clientele that visits Amazon to search for products and the population at large that is looking for the product, regardless of where it is warehoused or who is selling it. To be able to do that you have to engage in search engine optimization (SEO). And there are two kinds. You have to think about Google SEO to reach the world at large, and you have to think about Amazon SEO if you want to think about buyers who are Amazon-centric. We've laid both out here for you.

Google SEO

Although 65% of online buyers go to Amazon to buy the product that still leaves 35% of the market on the table. In a market that is $300 billion annually, leaving 35% on the table is nothing short of foolish. So what you need to do is promote your products through product reviews and websites. This is one of the best ways you can do this.

1. Register websites that are product specific. For instance, if you sell whip cream makers then get whipcreammakers.com or something like that. For search engine optimization a website with the product you are trying to promote does well. Therefore, if you have a large inventory of whip cream makers and someone keys in whip cream maker into a Google search engine box, you are aiming for the results to include your website in the top half of the page.

2. Get ghostwriters to write articles and review of the different whip cream makers that you offer and create a trove of articles that you can then

become a resource for people looking for the product.(Primary Site)
3. Have another set of writers write about the original site and send it out on social media. (Secondary Site)
4. Have a large Social Media presence and promote the Secondary Site.
5. Create an email database by giving away free eBooks or gifts and send your email recipients new articles from the Secondary site. This will start to increase the credibility of the secondary sites with Google that will, in turn, raise the profile of the Primary site.
6. Use PPC advertisements that target the Primary site based on keywords that are similar to your website's domain name. Keep the primary keywords similar or the domain name.
7. Keep updating your articles and product reviews on the primary site. Keep it fresh.
8. As you build your email database and your social media presence keep sending customers to the primary and secondary sites respectively. All this is purposed to increase your standing on the

search engine results page. When a potential buyer that is looking for your product searches for it in Google, you want them to get to your web page, and from there you can direct them to your Amazon sales page for that product.

Extra income: *If you really want to squeeze every penny out of this, then what you can do is join the Amazon affiliate program and use the affiliate links in your primary sites so that every time a visitor clicks on that link and makes a purchase, you will get the affiliate commission in addition to the profit on the product. Amazon does not consider this in poor tastes or does it violate anything in the FBA agreements. If you don't do it, you are actually leaving money on the table.*

Amazon SEO

The idea of SEO, as the term implies is to optimize the results of your product when a person does a search query using one of the search engines. We saw that with the Google SEO endeavors. However, there is one more database that you need to focus on in terms of being found on a search query. That is the Amazon search itself.

Remember we said earlier that 65% of online buyers search for the item on Amazon first. That is a huge reason to be in those search results. If you allow organic factors to slowly get your product to get to the top of the search results and you are going to find that it's probably never going to make it. The one thing that you have to understand is that there is more than one seller on Amazon that is selling the same product using FBA or fulfilling it themselves. In any case, your goal is to get your product in front of the customer on Amazon as many times as possible so that they have the opportunity to make the purchase. Think of it as shelf space in a grocery store. All products at eye level command a premium while those placed at ground level do not. It's the same reason you find generic brands that are significantly cheaper down there.

How does that translate to revenue at Amazon? It translates to increased revenue, in fact, because when you place the item at 'eye-level' or in the top search results, customers are more likely to pic k it than to go on searching. It is not human nature to find something they are looking to purchase and put it back and search for something else. This is especially true for someone who makes purchases without being sensitive to price – like Amazon Prime members. Now, are you starting to see how important this group is?

Back to Amazon SEO strategies.

Amazon's search engine algorithm is different from Google's. It differs in priorities and it differs in methodology so you can't use the same strategies that you used in trying to get your blogs and reviews ranked on Google. Instead, Amazon is highly sensitive to keywords. And that is the way you want to approach this. Put a significant amount of thought into how you describe your product.

Let me illustrate. If the ordinary surfer went to Google and keyed in 'cocoa'. What would you suppose they are looking for? Could they be in search of how to make cocoa? Or are they looking for cocoa to purchase? Or perhaps they are looking to see what cocoa is. There are so many possible intentions behind a Google search but not so in an Amazon search. You guessed it, there is only one intention (or two, if you include someone doing competitor analysis). As such, when Amazon receives a search they are looking specifically at a person looking to purchase an object. This makes your keyword strategy simpler and easier to execute.

Here is how you do it:

1. Find an Amazon keyword tool that offers free services or gets a premium one after you have tested its functionality.
2. Type in one keyword that you can think of for your product and the tool should be able to give you a list of keywords that Amazon relates to that initial word that you keyed it. Amazon does this based on an autocomplete feature, which in itself says a lot about the word you are searching.
3. From that list of keywords that you get, type in each result into a search box n Amazon and look at what product pops up in the results. Harvest what's relevant and discard the rest.
4. Make a list of all the relevant keywords and put it way for the moment
5. There are a number of parameters that you can control when you create the listing. Make sure you

use the keywords that describe the brand, the product and possibly the functionality in the title.

6. When you do this Amazon attaches keywords importance to three possible areas that your customer could be looking for that product that you are selling: manufacturer, function, and model. Let's say, for instance, if you wrote a title like this: Tramontina 24in Induction Cooker Stainless Steel Wok with Glass Cover, you have hit three key areas, so that whenever a customer is looking for something made by Tramontina, your product is going to figure into the results. When they search for Wok (product) you're going to get the possibility of a hit. When they search for Stainless Steel and Induction Cooker, it's going to get another hit. This will give it a lot of breadth – meaning it shows up for different kinds of searches. But what you also want altitude – how high up the results page your product shows up.

7. Titles and descriptions factor for a lot in keyword search results.

8. When you go back to the results that you picked in step 4, go back and chose the keywords that you missed or omitted and only look at the ones that are

relevant. For instance, you can remove Tramontina Knives as it is irrelevant to your objective.

Once you have accomplished this, you are ready to do the write up of your product n Amazon. Use the keywords that your competitors are using and place them strategically with importance on the titles and the description.

Once the product is listed make sure your website, primary and secondary sites are all active. For me, I typically give a way one or two gift cards for the specific redemption of the product as part of a raffle when people sign up with emails.

Therefore, if 1000 people sign up with an email I give the lucky random winner a free gift card to specifically buy that product with the condition that they leave a review. It will be positive because they got it for free. The reason for this is that you will start to get brownie points from both Google and Amazon because Google monitors search results and gives them higher importance if a person moves from search to site to Amazon and on to a successful purchase. It is a stamp of approval as far as Google is concerned that the customer found what he was looking for when he put in that search term. Your rankings get higher.

On Amazon's side they are monitoring the keyword that the customer used to get to your page and that prompts them to have more confidence in your product as well, but more importantly when you start to have good feedback scores right off the bat, it is weighted well in your favor. So the point at which you get the customer to flow from your site to Amazon and then gets your product and check out gives Amazon a stamp of approval for your product.

One of the best strategies on Amazon is to give away vouchers to a handful of people and extract email addresses from them.

Chapter 4 Hacks to Rank Better

Ok so, if nothing else, this is the chapter you need to pay the most attention to and this is the chapter that no one wants you to know about. This is the chapter that's going to show you how to pull off some of the craziest hacks in the history of Amazon and get your products in front of customers more times than you can imagine. This is going to be some black hat stuff to get your FBA world off to a fantastic start.

To get ahead on Amazon you already know how to go ahead and get a great supply chain whether it is outsourcing Virtual Assistants to go source for products or getting manufacturers in China to make and build stuff for you to sell. You also know that getting on to FBA and targeting Prime customers puts you in better stead than anything else. But, you need to put all that together and add to it some of the black hat tactics and strategies that are contained in this chapter.

The first thing you need to do is get a software called Scrapebox. This is not an illegal tool, but it is a very powerful one. It allows you to scrape an unlimited amount of key words from a number of sites including Amazon and Google as well as more than 20 other engines. This is a significant leg up for you if you want to make it in the retail arbitrage world. It costs about $100 for a lifetime license to place it on one machine.

I suggest you use the Azure cloud VPS and install your Scrapebox on that machine. If you do it at home the amount of traffic you generate is going to make your ISP highly irritated. But if you do it on the Azure VPS, you get speed and accuracy. The Azure VPS has a six month free trial period and after that six months of learning your way around Scrapebox and Azure, you will find that you are an expert at getting your keywords to the level you want them.

Once you have located the keywords you can search for blogs that have comments posted on them. Go find all these comments and see what people are saying about them, or use Scrapebox to find blogs that do not have comment restrictions placed and comment on as many blogs as you can.

One of the best ways to extract links to your primary and secondary site is to use comments in blogs by placing the

URL of the secondary site. By design, your secondary site should have more back links to it and more active commenting pointing to it. This will raise the value of the keywords that you are using.

As you increase the number of comments in the relevant keywords what you are doing is assuring Google that those blogs which are indexed for the keyword that you are going after.

I've also seen many people pay for comments. It's easy to do that. To get it started you can pay $1 per comment and you can get a number of people in any freelance portal like freelancer.com or upworks.com to do it. I have not personally done that myself but I have seen how effective it is to increase the rankings of the product and the seller. But take it slow. If the algorithms on Amazon think that things are not organic they may penalize you for it. And if you are going to do this then maybe you will also be into placing comments on blogs automatically. I haven't done that but I hear that it can be extremely effective. It can be done using Scrabeox as well.

Fine Tuning Titles

The strategy that really works well when it comes to placing the product in top search results is to modify the title and the work with a brand name that you add on to that title. For instance, if you call your FBA company Brilliant, then you take your product, like the Tramontina Wok and instead of just labeling it Tramontina 24in Induction Cooker Stainless Steel Wok with Glass Cover, you can label it Tramontina Brilliant 24in Induction Cooker Stainless Steel Wok with Glass Cover. This will benefit you by placing Brilliant (your company's name) in your Google ranking programs and in your Amazon ranking programs so that when you start to show in the front pages of Google, Amazon will also start to see your product as unique to what the other sellers are offering.

You can also play with other strategies but these strategies in this chapter should be enough to get you in front of more people than you would if you didn't strategize. Remember to also attack using social media. Whatever black hat or white hat strategy you use, remember never sell the product directly. No one goes to their twitter feed hoping they come across a stainless steel pan or a gold watch. If anything, they will consider it spam and wither block you or if they are too polite they will mentally block you out of their scan.

Focus

Always keep your focus on your product and how fast it's moving out your door. You need to keep a strong handle over when you put the product in Amazon's warehouse and how fast that inventory is moving. You need to stay aware of each product you have. That awareness needs to be either mental or via the use of software. Never take on more product and inventory without being able to focus on it. If you can't focus on it, make sure you get someone to focus on it for you. There must be daily attention paid to each product so that you always endeavor to get more of it, promote it and move it.

Chapter 5 Feedback and Ratings

We touched on this a little in the last two chapters. Now we are going to talk about it in detail. Feedback and ratings account for a lot in the Amazon world. If you are to succeed in this business it is going to be because Amazon gradually starts giving you more search results exposure and they will only do that if your ratings and comments are in good standing. Don't underestimate this, they have automated this and it works very well.

You must know that it is no longer permissible to have customers leave feedback in return for free stuff. There really isn't much you can do when it comes to trying to black hat comments for feedback. I would strongly discourage you from using underhanded means like paying someone to do it. It is definitely available. There are people who are paid to leave comments but if you get caught doing it, they will shut down your account. That is not worth the hassle. Paying for commenting on blogs is not the same thing as paying for feedback on Amazon's page. Bottom line: don't do it.

Instead, do it the old fashioned way. Give your customers the best service possible that they will be more than happy to leave you with stellar comments. Here are five ways that you could request customers to leave a positive comment.

1. Make sure that you give them a really good product. Mind you if the design of the product is not good, that is not your fault. I have found that leaving a free gift in the box or a surprise twofer in the packaging before sending it to Amazon is a great way to get customers to leave feedback. There is no penalty for you to leave more in the box than you advertise. You just can't leave less. When customers open the package and find they got more than they bargained for they will be pleasantly surprised. You could also leave a note in the package that congratulates them and asks them to take a moment and leave a rating for you. It works every time.
2. Make sure you have a very well written product description and that it is unique from the rest. If you have good pictures and great descriptions people are

more inclined to commend you for that in addition to the comments for the product.
3. Target Prime customers and leave a note in the description that says that you would love to hear from them so that you can make your offerings better by improving on the good and hanging the bad.
4. Let everyone know that they should comment on the delivery and on the product. Because these are two different things.
5. Remember that you don't want reviews just so that you have better sales. You can live on a prayer here. You want people to give you honest feedback so that you can take real steps to giving people what they want. If you are willing to walk the extra mile and do the right thing then you are going to be able to automatically get the reviews that will boost sales.

If you do get a poor feedback for whatever reason, be sure to take it seriously and work to resolve whatever complaints that the buyer described. Never just leave it unattended.

Chapter 6 Customer Loyalty Secrets

Just in case you haven't realized it yet the biggest part of customer loyalty has already been taken care of. Amazon already has one of the most popular and profitable customer loyalty programs and as much as they are the force that enables you to make the best out of an intentional business they don't want you to have the loyalty of the customer, they want to keep the loyalty of the customer to themselves.

No, I am not mocking them or speaking ill of them. It is their customer and they have every right to monopolize customer loyalty. I just want you to be absolutely clear about what's what. Most people forget that the customer doesn't belong to you. Have you noticed how they do not allow the customer to contact you or you, them? Of course, there are ways around it, but the barriers to entry are rather steep.

So what is the point of this entire chapter? Well, this entire chapter is for you to rethink the whole concept of customer loyalty. You need to get out from the traditional framework of personal customer relationship and customer acquisition strategies. There is none. Your customer acquisition strategy was signing up with Amazon. Your customer acquisition steps were getting the research into what product was needed and where you could cater to a niche.

Your job from here on out is to keep Amazon happy. How do you do that? You do that by keeping its customer's happy and by following the rules of the marketplace. As long as you do that then you will be treated well and treated preferentially to the extent of the possible limits.

This is the secret. To get great customer reviews, to be treated well by Amazon, to be a good community citizen there are three things you need to do:

1. Choose your products wisely and price them appropriately.
2. Delist products that do not sell and go back to the drawing board.
3. Follow the rules.

When you do this you will be able to keep your biggest customer happy. You do know who your biggest customer is, right? Your biggest customer is Amazon and they are the ones that you need to satisfy.

Conclusion

We started off this book by telling you what selling on Amazon's marketplace is about and what it is a not. If you can refocus your understanding of Amazon then you can start to recognize the strengths that come with it and how there is a symbiotic relationship between one of the largest marketplaces in the world and the small contributors that sell on it.

Your frame of mind to sell on Amazon should be one that only uses Amazon as a portal and fulfilling agent. You should endeavor to market your product heavily outside of that. For that purpose, you can engage a number of foot soldiers to do your work for you. The real beauty in the digital economy is that it grants you the opportunity to have each job done by an individual anywhere in the world; it allows you to use one expert to manufacture; another expert to store and ship; another expert to host the product and bring in the traffic.

In this list of things that need to happen, Amazon handles the site, markets the brand, brings in the people, supports customer service, warehouses the product and event restocks it in case of returns. On your part, you just have to sell the product and that's what you have to do. Do not think for one second that Amazon is going to sell the product for you. They won't.

The other thing that we stressed repeatedly is for you to keep your costs low. Lower costs in a market that are inelastic to price allows you to directly mount an assault on competitors. Remember costs and prices are two different things. Costs are what you pay for a product, the amount you pay to ship it to the final destination, and how much you pay to store it and restock it. I take costs across all my performing assets into account when I am using Amazon. This is important because if you think about it, how much you pay staff, how much you pay for Amazon's storage, and how much you pay your Virtual Assistants all come out of your gross earnings from Amazon. As such you should think of all of them as cost centers and endeavor to keep them as low as possible.

The more strategic your thinking, the further you will advance with Amazon. Markets that are this large and that are fluid require strategic moves and tactical advances. You cannot just ram your way through and hope to make a buck for very long. The road to success is littered on both sides with those who tried to wing it.

The opportunities FBA affords you are not static by any means. You can start with FBA with just a few products, then build that up and add on larger products or custom made products that you can do via merchandiser fulfillment and then you can increase the volume of your offering by putting on goods that you manufacture. The opportunities are there if you just decide to think about it and invest your time and funds into expanding your exposure.

As you contemplate an FBA thrust forward, consider this as well: FBA is should not be and was never designed to be, a one channel strategy. Those who do well with Amazon are using multiple sales channels to get their products out in front of the customer and using Amazon as a way to complete the purchase and perfect the transaction. There are certainly spillover effects and that causes some sellers who have one or two products to make a sale here and there, but that should not be the extent of your overall strategy. I know someone who was trying out the FBA avenue and just listed one product and followed that up with zero marketing and did not use any other channels. The product did not sell during the time he had it listed.

One of the ways that you can actively sell is to have online websites that promote your products or your brand. If you do this then you will be able to leverage your position on Amazon. Think about that for a second. If you generate sales outside of Amazon and you bring a buyer to purchase through Amazon then you profit and you are able to generate feedback. As you build on that feedback, more Amazon-centric customers will be exposed to your offering. It works both ways. But the key that you take a way with you is that you must actively dominate the search engine results if you are going to be able to make this a success.

Invest in the software you need to make your efforts pay off. These apps generally magnify your efforts by making your returns larger and they always pay for themselves. You just need to stay persistent.

Every game you play has traps. In golf, there are sand traps, just as in chess there are traps as well. Amazon is no different. There are major traps that you need to keep an eye out for. These traps are not intentionally set out by someone in the hopes to get you violated. No, these traps are the rules and the nature of the environment.

On the one hand, there are rules that you have to abide by. You have to follow marketplace rules set out by Amazon and those rules need to be followed or else you could find yourself suspended with inventory tied up in warehouses and cash tied up in accounts. Not only should you not intentionally break the rules, you should make sure you know what all the rules are so you do not land up accidentally infringing them.

There is a certain ecosystem that is at play here on the Amazon marketplace. You need to know your environment like the back of your hands. To do that you need to do is read the entire set of rules and regulations of the Amazon marketplace before you fall afoul of any of them without intending to do so.

The second trap that you need to identify and understand is that if you are not ready to do the necessary keyword search, to identify and source low-cost products and to be able to promote your products successfully, then you are entering a trap where you will lose money.

If you are just starting out, the only advice anyone can offer you is that you keep at it and keep improving how you go about it. The tips and strategies to hack Amazon are in here, you just need to get up and put it to good use.

www.ingramcontent.com/pod-product-compliance
Lightning Source LLC
Chambersburg PA
CBHW050018230526
45470CB00003B/1022